The ABCs of Leadership

The ABCs of Leadership

Leading God's Way

Shirley J. Jones

Kingdom Living Publishing
Accokeek, MD

Published by:

Kingdom Living Publishing
P.O. Box 660
Accokeek, MD 20607

Published in the United States of America.

ISBN 978-0-9968089-3-4

Dedication

Dedicated to the first Leadership Class of Rehoboth Family Life Center: There is greatness, destiny, and purpose in each one of you. I so look forward to your journey and the mark you will make upon the earth as leaders for Christ!

Acknowledgments

I give thanks:

To God: I continue to stand in awe of God, and I am so grateful to Him for everything.

To my family: Jamal, Taihra, Madison, Nigel, and Nylah; Hasan, Angel, Manuel, and Laila—I am blessed.

To my church family: Rehoboth Family Life Center—church not as usual. I am so honored and excited about all of you and your purpose and destiny.

To my encouragers: For all the words of encouragement, support, and pushing forward from friends who keep my ears attuned to God; especially Apostle Saundra Hagans who covers the ministry and Elder Vera Jackson, with whom I share the sentiment, "Just keep it moving."

To Pastor Irma McKnight: You are the best of the best in so many areas of my life. I pray a hundred-fold blessing for all that you have done for my family and me; and for always having a "you can do it" for me.

Table of Contents

Foreword

I first met Shirley Jones about thirty-two years ago at a church we both attended. Little did I know that God had orchestrated our meeting and would allow us to become covenant sisters. During the earlier years, we would walk the track at a local high school and spend time sharing the Word of God over the telephone. At one time, we found ourselves in very similar situations and took turns encouraging each other, not realizing perhaps that there was a much greater picture, and that the tests we were enduring were intended to bring us to a greater place for a greater purpose.

Since that time, Shirley Jones has become a woman of faith, courage, excellence, and wisdom. She is now known as Apostle Shirley Jones and Senior Pastor; I must say, with all honesty, she pastors according to the heart of God. She ministers with love and is very liberal when it comes to allowing the rivers to flow from her onto others.

I am honored to call her my friend and confidant and am so very proud of all she has accomplished during her years of ministry. I believe she is one of God's best-kept secrets in the D.C. area (soon to be exposed).

If you are in leadership in any capacity, and you want to sharpen your leadership skills, conduct a leadership training workshop, or if you're looking for an excellent book on how to effectively lead and instruct a people, well you are holding in your hand the tool necessary to meet those leadership training needs. After utilizing this book, expect to see change in those you have trained.

Apostle Saundra L. Hagans
Senior Pastor,
Covenant House of God Church
Philadelphia, PA

Preface

I was on my way to church, and the Lord spoke to me about writing a book in 90 days. My first reaction was that 90 days was just not enough time. Then I thought about a small pamphlet that I had done for our women's retreat the year before; I had been talking about developing it into a book. I was now okay with the 90-day time frame since at least the making of a few chapters were done.

During the message that morning the Holy Spirit had me encourage a few people to write the books that they had within them, record the compact disc of songs they had written and sung, and just operate in the gift they were given. Ron, a member of the church, was thinking about writing a book and using some previous things he had already written. I was led during the message to go into covenant with him for both of us to have books to the publisher within 90 days. We high fived and touched and agreed.

Then it all changed. I did not start working immediately on the book since part of it was already done, and a lot of things were taking place in the month of October. At the beginning of November, the Lord began to speak to me about a leadership manual. I was given a name for the manual; I saw the cover; and I was given instructions to write about an aspect of leadership every day, except Sunday, for six weeks. I was also instructed to get loose-leaf paper, a notebook, dividers, pens, and high lighters. I was to take a Divine Leadership Class and write what I heard so that others could be developed as leaders. Thus, this leadership manual has been divinely given by God that you may lead and make disciples, and even stand out in the marketplace as one who can bring about change.

I am totally in awe of the faithfulness of God. When I came before Him every day as He had instructed me to do; He spoke the words that are written in these pages. I have sat in the classroom of God, and I pray the words He spoke will cause you to be the best you are called to be.

This manual is yours to read, reflect, and pray. Let the classroom of leadership begin now. Be blessed as I have been blessed.

Lessons

Instructions

This manual covers different principles of leadership that were divinely given by God. The Lord has also instructed me to share my woes and victories in becoming a leader. Although the principles are biblically based, they can be utilized in the marketplace as well.

To get the most out of this manual, study one principle at a time. Pray the prayer at the end of the section along with what is in your heart. Use the "Notes/Reflections" page to write where you are in what you just read. Think on those daily encounters where you could have walked in a leadership principle; or where you felt a tug of the Holy Spirit on your heart and ignored it. What caused you to not move? After studying the principle, if given the same or similar opportunity, how would you handle it?

I pray that as you move through the manual and begin applying the principles, the leader in you will emerge, even the more, the way God tells you to lead. Prepare yourself to be opened, corrected, instructed, and then launched forward as an ambassador of Christ, the salt of the earth, and the light of the world. Lead!

A

Be an Encourager

Never assume that people do not need a word of encouragement regardless of who they are and in what position they sit. We never know what is going on in the life of people. Example: While walking to get on the train one morning, I saw a woman who was dressed very stylishly. She got on the escalator in front of me, but we arrived at the top about the same time. I felt a stirring to say something, so I mentioned that she was a very classy lady and looked nice. She stopped and thanked me and said, "You do not know how much I needed to hear that." I was so thankful that I went with what was in my spirit. Know that a lot of things you have experienced were to make you able to encourage others to see and know God is faithful and He will bring them through. Sometimes it is the small things we say or do that may make the difference in a bad day versus a good day, leaving the church or staying, or even committing suicide or becoming determined to live.

As a leader, you must be willing to speak words of encouragement, even when they may not always be received. I believe when God places something on your heart to speak to someone, it will make a difference. Let us, as leaders, just be obedient to the stirring of encouraging words. Somebody encouraged and pushed you. Now do it for someone else that they may become all that God has planned for them to become.

I watch people blossom into their gift and calling when words of life have been spoken to them. I thank God for all the people who have encouraged me to move forward and do the things I am doing now in my life and those things still yet to come.

I speak words of encouragement to you as the leader in you is further birthed out of you and that you make a difference in the places you are called to lead. The people are further waiting to hear your encouraging words as they are being crafted by the Holy Spirit. Open up your mouth, Encourager!

Prayer

As a leader, Father, allow me to be an encourager to those You place before me. Let me be sensitive to the needs of others and the move of the Spirit within me. Let my tongue be used to speak words of life. So many people have encouraged me; now let me do it for somebody else. Thank You for the opportunity to do so! Amen.

Notes/Reflections

B

Do Not Be Afraid to Lead

Do not be afraid to lead. One of the hardest places to lead is where you have been taken out from among men. Remember Jesus in Luke 4:24 said, *"Assuredly I say unto you, no prophet is accepted in his own country."* This principle is twofold. You see you as one of them, and they see you as one of them. Now you are called to stand in a leadership position over the folks who hung with you and served with you.

"Have I not commanded you? Be strong and of a good courage; do not be afraid, nor be dismayed, for the Lord your God is with you wherever you go" (Joshua 1:9). There are some lines that you will have to draw gradually. Draw them. Some people will not understand, and others may think that you have become arrogant, but for their sake and yours, this must take place.

I recall this word being spoken to me by God:

"Let Me teach you how to lead—not make best friends (if that happens, fine) but lead. Your intentions are not to offend but know that what you say and do may cause offense. Let Me work this out. Just follow My lead as you

lead. Remember I have called you to this post, so let me do it. Your job is to stay before Me; receive so that what you have can be filtered to the group you are leading. Remember, as the leader, there are some things that I am only going to tell you. There will be confirmation but what if there is not? I still spoke it so what are you going to do? Do what and how I say to do it. You set the tempo and the direction. Stay ever before Me. People will always have opinions and sometimes it maybe outside of what you have heard Me speak. Thank them for their opinion, but do what I told you to do. Weigh it and stay open, but at the end of the day, I will have the final word for you. Lead. Do not play down your role. Lead."

Servant leader—Jesus came to serve and not to be served. Do not micro lead. Your hands do not need to be in everything. Place people in positions to exercise their gifting and dedication (unto Him) and let them do it. Always stay in the loop and have answers. Do not be caught not knowing what is going on. Know the pulse of the thing. Pick the places that you use your authority to bring about changes.

Make leaders where you lead; do not become possessive where you think you are the only one that can do that thing. Not so!

Do not be afraid to move or sit people down. This is about Kingdom building. Lead and make leaders!

Prayer

Father God, cause me to settle into the place of leadership that You have ordained for me. Help me to keep my focus on You and heed the instructions that You are giving explicitly to me. I yield myself totally to You. Teach and lead me, Father God, and I will continue to give You praise, honor, and glory forevermore. Amen!

Notes/Reflections

_____

_____

_____

_____

_____

_____

_____

_____

_____

_____

_____

_____

_____

_____

_____

_____

_____

_____

_____

C

Lead by Example

True leaders are first partakers of the words taught, preached, or instructions given. We as leaders especially need not be hearers of the word only, but doers as well. God will cause us to get a true witness in the area we are being prepared to lead even when we are not aware that we are being exercised for that very purpose. If not, then we become hypocrites like the Pharisees and Sadducees of old. I always say I would never ask anyone to do something that I was not willing to do and have not done. *But I discipline my body, and bring it into subjection, lest, when I have preached to others, I myself should become disqualified* (1 Corinthians 9:27).

Lead by example. Let what you ask be demonstrated in you.

Prayer

Lord, let Your Word that You give me find me out first that I not be a hypocrite and walk in false humility. Let my life be a demonstration of what I speak daily. Thank You, Lord. Amen.

Notes/Reflections

D

Be Willing to Share Your Stuff

I have learned that many things that I have gone through or experienced—the good, bad and ugly—have given me a sense of
compassion and caused me not to be judgmental. As a leader, we
must not forget from whence we have come and remember but
by the grace of God there go I. There are things about which only
you and God know. Never get puffed up or think you have arrived.
Pride goes before destruction and a haughty spirit before a fall
(Proverbs 16:18).

Be willing to allow God to spill you as He wills. We feel that
people do not need to know our stuff, but we really do not have any
stuff, if everything belongs to God. He will place you before people
experiencing what you came from or out of to let them know that
they can come out with victory too because of Him. *There is no
respect of person* (Colossians 3:25b). Whatever God did for you,
He can do it for them.

When you are willing to share some stuff as God directs you
with wisdom to do so, people can see you as themselves, approach-
able and human. *For we have not an high priest which cannot be
touched with the feeling of our infirmities; but was in all points*

tempted like as we are, yet without sin. Let us therefore come boldly unto the throne of grace, that we may obtain mercy, and find grace to help in time of need (Hebrews 4:15-16). Your victory in your stuff helps to solidify what you say. People wonder or even ask, "How do you know?" Then your response can be, "How much time do you have?" This becomes your open door to share.

Do not be afraid to share your current stuff and mistakes. We need to understand that there will be a perfecting until we leave the earth. Throughout the Bible, people who did great things for God had stuff, but they learned how to get before God and repent. David was a murderer and committed adultery, but God called him a man after His own heart. Paul asked God three times to remove the thorn that was in his flesh and was told, "But My grace is sufficient." Hopefully, this will stop people from making you a saint and placing wings on your back. We are not perfect, but willing to do what God instructs us to do.

Leaders hurt, cry, are disappointed, scared, and experience a slew of emotions that everybody else does, except we learn to get before God and allow His love to satiate our very being. If we are not doing this, then we need to begin to do so now.

Prayer

Father, help me to be willing as You direct to share my mistakes with others. Let me not walk in pride and try to project that I have always walked upright before You. For if that were the truth, then there would not have been a need for Calvary. I pray now that my mistakes and Your forgiveness cause me to move with compassion as a leader. I have no stuff, but I am transparent before You and before the people. I am so forgiven. Thank You!

Notes/Reflections

_____

_____

_____

_____

_____

_____

_____

_____

_____

_____

_____

_____

_____

_____

_____

_____

_____

_____

_____

_____

_____

E

Count the Cost to Lead

Count the cost. *For everyone to whom much is given, from him much will be required; and to whom much has been committed, of him they will ask the more* (Luke 12:48b). It is going to cost you to be a leader in the Kingdom of God. You may, no you will, lose sleep and friends, be misunderstood. There will be disappointments; name slandered, accusations of saying things that you didn't say, people trying to get close to you just because you are a leader. Your body, mind, finances, household, job and everything else that encompasses your life will come under attack from the enemy. You will be under the eyes of onlookers and those jockeying for your position. Some will think that you are not qualified or capable of being in your role of leadership and that they could do a better job; some will tell you so and tell others as well. You must set boundaries for what and where you can go, do, and say and spend energy.

You are probably wondering and asking yourself why me? Reason: Because He said so and asked you to be a part of His plan of redemption and because we win.

People see what they view as the glitz and glamor of ministry; people know your name and who you are; you get invited to important stuff, wear nice clothes, and sit on the front row. In the scheme of things, these things do not amount to a hill of beans. You will be asked to do things you would just rather not and deal with people with whom you would rather not deal.

I remember God presented a situation to me, but I just did not want to deal with the person involved. I did not say anything, but He scanned my heart (He does this), and in the middle of the night He asked me, "Should I look for another?" Wow! I was outdone and felt bad. I repented and told God I would contact the person as directed. It really did not have anything to do with them, but God was looking for my obedience in this situation and beyond. The call on my life was based on obedience. If I could not obey here, then I could not move forward in what God was calling for my life. Upon reaching out to the person as directed, I found that encounter to be different from our previous encounter, and it was a blessing in my life. We must trust God with everything and know that He has our best interest at heart.

In the Garden of Gethsemane, Jesus said, *"If it is possible, let this cup pass from Me; nevertheless, not as I will, but as You will"* (Matthew 26:39). Jesus moved outside of Himself to do what He knew He was called to do. Rejoice in that because He did, we have a chance to live and be used by God. Know what you are called to do; stay before God and let Him direct and keep you.

It is not easy, but easy only gets you embers. You want and need the fire of the anointing of the Holy Spirit. Count the cost and know that we win!

Prayer

Father, help me to stay ever before you and not be moved by anything or anyone but You. It is You that called me for a time such as this, and I pray that all grace will abound in me, Your servant. Indeed, greater is He that is within me than he that is in the world. I win! Hallelujah! Amen!

Notes/Reflections

F

Manage Your Time

Learn to manage your time. Do not allow people to dictate your time or selfishly take up your time. Not everything is an emergency, and it all does not need to be done now. God created everything in six days and on the seventh day He rested. We must allow God to instruct us on how to manage our days. *There remains therefore a rest for the people of God (*Hebrews 4:9*).* There must be a balance in our lives according to Proverbs 11:1 (KJV), "A *false balance is abomination to the Lord: but a just weight is His delight."* We must spend time in prayer and the Word and have quiet time to be effective in leadership. Jesus separated Himself and went away to pray and have time alone.

Good things and right things that are done at the wrong time are just wrong. Listen for when. *Be anxious for nothing, but in everything by prayer and supplication, with thanksgiving, let your requests be made known to God; and the peace of God, which surpasses all understanding, will guard your hearts and minds through Christ Jesus* (Philippians 4:6-7).

When I give my day over to God, I get all things done and have time left over. Let Him lead and guide you. Do not be afraid to say, "I can't right now." Do not overload yourself. You will burn out and will not want anything to do with ministry. *The steps of a righteous man are ordered by the Lord and He delighteth in his way* (Psalm 37:23 KJV).

Prayer

Father God, your Word tells me that the steps of a righteous man are ordered by You. Help me to follow Your lead in everything that I do. I surrender my life anew and afresh today, and I acknowledge You as being Lord of my life and all of my days. Lead me so that You are pleased with me and I am where I need to be according to Your will and plan for my life. Amen

Notes/Reflections

_____
_____
_____
_____
_____
_____
_____
_____
_____
_____
_____
_____
_____
_____
_____
_____
_____
_____
_____
_____
_____
_____
_____
_____

G

Be the You God Has Made

A good leader respects and follows the authority figure of the house but does not lose the uniqueness of who he or she is and how the job is done. I remember being ordained with three other people and all of them had undergraduate degrees and even master degrees. Here I stood coming from Philadelphia with still a lot of slang being a part of my vocabulary. I started to watch myself closely as I watched and listened to them. I struggled with presenting each time because I was not being who I truly was. Finally, the Holy Spirit let me know that God knew who I was, slang and all, when He called me to the office of Pastor. Moreover, if it did not bother or stop Him, why was I bothered? He let me know that if there were anything that needed to be changed, He would quicken me or He would just change it. I felt better and could relax and just be me. Be you and be the best you can be!

There are people that only you can reach because of who you are, where you have been, and where you are from. That is why you were called. Do not alter who you are so that your witness will not become null and of no effect.

Do not allow people to put you in a box and especially not their box. Do not play down your gift because of anyone. Honor God by using the gifts and talents that He has given you. He really does expect a return on the gifts. Be in a place where your gifts can be exercised and use them in all areas of your life: work, church, home, relationships, etc.

Do not force or try to make anything happen. Your gift will make room for you. God will open up the opportunity for your gift to be known. At a previous church, I was asked to open up Bible Study in prayer; then the following Sunday I was asked to open up the service in prayer. The Pastor said that clearly there was an anointing on my life and he would draw every gift out of me. I started out teaching the children. Later, I was placed over the Education Department for adults and children. I taught Bible Study, codevelop new members and new believers' classes, taught spiritual gift class, and served on the board of directors and the women's steering committee. After I was ordained, I served as the Assistant Pastor and preached on those Sundays when the pastor was out of town and whenever he requested me to do so, and I answered church related questions and counseled members. In the midst of all of this, I wrote my first book "*Intimacy with God.*" All of these places and duties were establishing me for the position where I stand today. It is a process and journey as God continues to shape and mold you for His purpose. Let Him do it.

Prayer

Father, You knew me even before I was formed in my mother's womb. You know my thoughts afar off. You know everything about me. I pray that You will continue to shape and mold me according to Your plan. I am the clay, and You are the potter. I fashion myself after no one except the image of the Trinity that You declared at the beginning of time. I want You to be pleased with me. I am quiet before you today. Father have your way in and through me. I bless Your name. Amen!

Notes/Reflections

_____

_____

_____

_____

_____

_____

_____

_____

_____

_____

_____

_____

_____

_____

_____

_____

_____

_____

_____

_____

_____

_____

H

Know Those That Labor with You

Know those that labor with you. Get to know those with whom you lead and work in the ministry, their gifts, passions, likes, and dislikes. Strive for unity among the body. Psalm 133 tells us where there is unity God commands blessings forevermore.

When you are in a battle, you need to know who will stay on the wall and not be moved, who will not be afraid to draw their weapon and shoot, who has the gift of healing, who moves in the prophetic accurately, and who can see in the spirit first. All are needed to get where you need to be.

Do not allow the enemy to cause contention and strife between you and your brother or sister. Work it out and talk it out. A lot of times, it is about perception and not even reality. I remember someone asking me if we were okay, meaning them and me; and my reply was yes. When I asked them why they asked me that, their reply was because I came up the aisle and did not speak to them. I told them, "When you see me going up the aisle, I am usually headed to check on things or to put out a fire. I don't even see you. If there is an issue, I will let you know." Will people sometimes rub you the wrong way? Yes, but sit before God until nothing moves within you when you are in the person's presence. Give the enemy no place in your soul.

God will show you to whom to bare your soul. Let God show you and do not choose based on some criteria that are not of God. Our choosing is so surfaced, but God is sure.

Learn to celebrate one another knowing that we have a season to go forth, differently but going forth. *For where two or three are gathered together in My name, I am there in the midst of them* (Matthew 18:20).

Push your sister and brother so that you all win!

Prayer

Father, help me never to be an instrument of the enemy to cause contention and strife among the brethren, but to walk in love and to get to know those who I labor with for You. Let me forever be mindful of me at all times. Show me when I need to be recalibrated for your purpose. Help me dear Lord to celebrate my brothers and sisters and push them forth in destiny. Keep me pure and keep us pure, in Jesus' name. Amen!

Notes/Reflections

I

Do Things Decently and In Order

Do things decently and in order. When you do not know, ask. Always be mindful of the leadership that has been put in place by God. Never assume anything. If there are questions, ask. If you are in key positions of leadership, you should let your leaders know you will not be in attendance for a service or function, especially if you play a part in the worship service.

Leaders should never try to lord authority over you, or have you do everything that they want you to do for the sake of just wanting to have you do it. They should not be walking in a spirit of 'serve me, serve me.' It is not necessary for them to give you permission to visit another church or ministry. This causes control and bondage, which is not of God.

Follow the leader as he or she follows Christ.

Never leave out of the back door, if possible. I believe that people come in to be healed, set free, discover their gift(s), be exercised in their gift, and possibly move on to work out their purpose and destiny. Knowing this principle keeps leaders from taking it personally.

Stay open to the move of God and do not be afraid to move, if need be. There may be another impression that a house of worship somewhere else has what you need to be further equipped. Pray about your moves. God is a God of order. He would not cause confusion on your part. You cannot be responsible for the reaction of another person. Check you first, always!

Prayer

You are a God of Order. Father, please do not allow me to react or respond out of my flesh, but move in the Spirit. Allow me to be a blessing and not a hindrance in the positions you place me. Help me always to examine myself and be a servant leader each day. I want to serve the people of God even in my leading. Thank you, Lord. Amen.

Notes/Reflections

_____
_____
_____
_____
_____
_____
_____
_____
_____
_____
_____
_____
_____
_____
_____
_____
_____
_____
_____
_____
_____
_____

J

Not about You but God

Remember that this is about God and not you. You have been called to be a part of God's plan of redemption. Therefore, it is God who will instruct you and give you everything that you will need to lead. You will not have to try to make anything happen; just let God be God. You do not possess the things to lead in the way of the Kingdom.

Build Me a house, and I will come. Just before I moved from the church where I was ordained, I taught a Bible Study entitled "Build Me a House and I Will Come." Five years later, I heard the phrase in my spirit. I discussed what I was sensing with my best friend, with whom I cofounded and co-directed an outreach ministry. We began to pray, and both of us received in our spirits that we were being given the charge to start a church. Things began to turn quickly. We were given a date for the first service—six weeks, no members, no place, and very little money. We were then given the name of the Church—Rehoboth Family Life Center. We searched for a place, but either nothing fit or space was not available. Finally, the Holy Spirit said, "Private schools." I began an internet search for private schools and the one where we now hold our services popped up. When I saw the picture of the school, I had a feeling that was the place, because it looked so much like the place we were using for our men and women's Bible studies and other outreach events. The administrators at the school mentioned that they had never rented out space, but that did not mean that it could not be done. They went to their board of directors, who approved our use of the space. Within six weeks, we opened the door for our first service, and five people joined that very first Sunday. We witnessed the faithfulness of the Almighty God! We stand in awe even now knowing that we stand in the plan of God.

We are called to be an ambassador representing the one that is sending us forth. We are the salt of the earth and light of the world. Jesus constantly said that He only did and said what the Father instructed Him to do and say.

Let this mind be in you, which was also in Christ Jesus, who, being in the form of God, did not consider it robbery to be equal with God, but made Himself of no reputation, taking the form of a bondservant, and coming in the likeness of men. And being found in appearance as a man, He humbled Himself, and became obedient to the point of death, even the death of the cross (Philippians 2:5-8).

Let us die to self and allow the Spirit of God to be the leader within us.

Prayer

Father God, I yield myself over to You and die to self and allow You to teach me the ways of the Kingdom. Through You Father, all things are possible. Be pleased with me in how I love and lead Your people. Continue to show me where I fall short and show me the righteous path to take. Your will and not my will be done. In Jesus' name, Amen!

Notes/Reflections

_____
_____
_____
_____
_____
_____
_____
_____
_____
_____
_____
_____
_____
_____
_____
_____
_____
_____
_____
_____

K

Don't Quit

Don't quit! How do you stop and sit down on what God has called for your life? Did God make a mistake?

I remember a pastor sent me an email with words of wisdom. She told me never to quit ministry on Sunday because by Monday evening it will be better. There are going to be times when folks (even in the church), circumstances, and being tired may cause you to consider throwing in the towel and going back to whatever you used to do and be. *Do you not know that those who run in a race all run, but one receives the prize? Run in such a way that you may obtain it* (1 Corinthians 9:24). God did not make a mistake; it is you that He has chosen for this position.

Let us run with endurance the race that is set before us, looking unto Jesus the author and finisher of our faith (Hebrews 12:1b-2a). Since He called you, He has everything that you need and will do everything necessary for you to accomplish the task over which He has called you to be a leader. It is about God, but for the people. God must be first in everything you do and say.

Prayer

Father, thank You for choosing me to lead in this position. I take it as an honor and privilege to be used by You. Father God, continue to strengthen me, give me perseverance, and allow me to rest in You when the times are trying, and I am weary. It was not easy for Your Son to go to the cross, but He did it for me. Help me to continue to move forward in thanksgiving to You and be a blessing to others. I press into You, dear Lord, for everything that I need. In Jesus' name. Amen.

Notes/Reflections

L

Stay Open to God

As a leader, grow and be willing to grow even out of your current position of leadership into another that God will call and place you in.

I think about when I led a daily prayer line early on, taught Bible Study, got ordained to the office of Pastor, assigned the role of Assistant Pastor, and assumed other responsibilities in the church. At work, I led customer service training and projects, assigned and did other training, etc. Then, build Me a house, and I will come. Now Senior Pastor of Rehoboth Family Life Center and affirmed as an Apostle. Wow! It just keeps evolving, and I know that there is still more to come.

Stay open to what God would have you to do for the furthering of the Kingdom. I pray for you that the gifts would continually be stirred up within you for purpose and destiny. *Verily, verily, I say unto you, He that believeth on Me, the works that I do shall he do also; and greater works than these shall he do; because I go unto My Father* (John 14:12 KJV).

Prayer

Father God, I say yes to my journey with You. Whatever, whenever, however, my answer is yes because my life is in Your hand. I
am grateful and look forward with You, the author and finisher of
my faith. In Jesus' name, Amen!

Notes/Reflections

_____

_____

_____

_____

_____

_____

_____

_____

_____

_____

_____

_____

_____

_____

_____

_____

_____

_____

_____

_____

_____

_____

_____

M

Love

Love must lead everything we do. I learned early on how much God loved me with all my mess, so how could I hold someone in disdain because of what they did to me? Love, His love, is what began the process of my life being put back together and me realizing I was going to be all right. My life was falling apart; I was making dumb choices and decisions, and I had no answers to make things better. Attending my son's program at a Christian school allowed me to hear something I did not understand, but it felt different. I started going to the church where the school was located on Sundays and Wednesdays and began to look forward to hearing more of the Word. When I surrendered to this call within me, His love started my journey to me becoming whole. He would tell me how much He loved me and how special I was to Him. He loved me so. Finally, one day I felt special and knew He loved me, and everything was going to be all right. His love covered all my sins and began to give me revelations about me, about Him, and about mankind. Seeing my sins, I realized that man, without God being at the helm of his life, is capable of anything. By the grace of God there go I and through no goodness of my own. I learned to love because He first loved me.

Read and study the love chapter in the Bible (1 Corinthians 13).

Hatred stirs up strife: but love covers all sins (Proverbs 10:12).

Love somebody whole.

Prayer

Father, I thank You so much for loving me and calling me unto Yourself. It was You loving me past my bad choices and mistakes and letting me know how special I was to You. I did not feel special; I felt undone and a mess. Nevertheless, You kept wooing me, and finally one day I could agree with You that I was special and I was going to be okay. Help me to love those You are calling me to lead. Let Your love flow from me to them and that they too will know how special they are and that they have purpose and destiny. Your love is all consuming. Amen!

Notes/Reflections

N

Know the Voice of God

You must know the voice of God. You are going to hear yourself, the enemy, and God. You need to know which is which. Do not entertain the voice or thoughts given by the enemy. *Casting down vain imaginations and every high thing that exalteth itself against the knowledge of God and bringing into captivity every thought to the obedience of Christ* (2 Corinthians 10:5). Satan is the father of lies, and there is no truth in him. Trust and obey God. *Howbeit when He, the Spirit of truth is come, He will guide you into all truth* (John 16:13).

I remember early on being at a church service, and the preacher gave an altar call for a woman that was going through in her marriage and household. He also mentioned one or two other things. What he said fit my situation, so I went to the altar for prayer along with another woman. When I left the church, I was bothered. The Holy Spirit played back the altar call directions. Yes, I fit some of what was said, but not all, and the call was very specific. It was for the other woman, not me. The Holy Spirit used this situation to teach me to listen to what is being said and listen to and for the voice of God. Hallelujah! *And when he brings out his own sheep, he goes before them; and the sheep follow him, for they know his voice* (John 10:4).

Prayers

Father, help me to hear and know Your voice that I may follow after You and You alone. Help me to continue to build a relationship with You to know Your ways and be able to discern what I hear. I lend my ears to You to hear Your instructions and wisdom to lead. Thank You, Father God. Amen!

Notes/Reflections

_____
_____
_____
_____
_____
_____
_____
_____
_____
_____
_____
_____
_____
_____
_____
_____
_____
_____
_____
_____
_____
_____
_____
_____

O

Take Responsibility

A good leader is going to make mistakes and miss some things. The worst mistakes are the ones from which we do not learn. Trust me; you will get another shot at it. Never point or place blame on others that are under your leadership. A leader must be a leader and take the responsibility of leading and bearing the burden of things not being done or not done correctly. Your job as a leader is to stay before God, receive instructions from Him, and filter it down to those you have been assigned to lead.

Do not wait for others to do or suggest. Lead. Lead even when it seems outweighed by others, once you get directions from God. At the end of the day, you must give an account to God for what you were instructed to do. You were instructed.

Big black shoes—big black boots—unlace the boots. I kept seeing these big black shoes. I finally asked God what it meant. He said they were the shoes of the Pastor. Wow! I shared this vision and revelation with a member of our church, who was a Lieutenant Colonel in the army. Later, she brought me a pair of jump boots that were laced up to the top. I took them home and placed them in my office so I could see them and be further reminded of the arduous responsibility of a pastor. The Holy Spirit instructed me to unlace the strings to the bottom, and He would instruct when to lace them up again. After having a week of hard decisions and having to make corrections, I was instructed to lace up two rows. I am still learning and becoming, and the boots are there before me as I wait to lace up another row.

Prayer

Father, I pray like Solomon that You give me wisdom and understanding to lead those You are assigning me to lead. Help me to remember, I am a leader and to lead. Help me to stay ever so close to You that I may know what to do in every given situation. I realize as the head goes the body follows. I yield myself to You, Father. The leader in me is whom You have called forth. I shall lead as You direct. Thank You. Amen!

Notes/Reflections

P

Stay Ever before God

As a leader, stay ever before the Lord. *Search me, O God, and know my heart; try me, and know my anxieties; and see if there is any wicked way in me, and lead me in the way everlasting* (Psalm 139:23-24). Our desire is or shall be to be right before God. *"The heart is deceitful above all things, and desperately wicked; who can know it? I, the Lord, search the heart, I test the mind, even to give every man according to his ways, according to the fruit of his doings* (Jeremiah 17:9-10). Let us not assume we are at a place, but let God, the one that knows everything about us, tell us.

I remember when the Lord told me that I was not surrendered yet. I was so upset because I thought I was. He began to show me areas that were not given over to Him. He loved me so, and I was willing to allow the work of righteousness to go deeper down within me. I am glad He does not leave us half-undone; there will be a working done in us until we leave the earth. We should never think that we have arrived and have our angel wings. Not!

Holy Spirit will at times replay your response or actions to show you your wrong responses and actions. Be thankful for the correction. *"My son, do not despise the chastening of the Lord, nor be discouraged when you are rebuked by Him: For whom the Lord loves He chastens, and scourges every son whom He receives"* (Hebrew 12:5b-13).

If God be pleased with me...

Prayer

Father, search me and the places that are not pleasing to You and will prevent me from being a valuable leader. First, show me and then rid me of them. You know me much better than I know the inner workings of my heart. I want You to be pleased with me, and I desire to be a blessing to the people. I yield and surrender myself to You. You are the potter, and I am the clay. Do with me whatever is fitting for You. I will forever give You praise. Amen!

Notes/Reflections

Q

Appreciate Others

As a leader, continue to let others know how much they are appreciated. We are blessed to have people at Rehoboth that serve and will do whatever is asked to cause things to run smoothly. They are also faithful watchmen on the wall. A good leader is one that people respect and join to complete a given task. Without good people working together things would not happen or continue to move forward. As you get to know your team, be creative in showing them how much they are appreciated. Never take anyone or anything for granted. From the smallest gesture to the largest, always say thanks. God appreciates them, so should you. No team, no need for a leader.

Esteem them very highly in love for their work's sake (1 Thessalonians 5:13a).

<u>Prayers</u>

Lord, allow me always to be mindful of others for what and how they contribute to the whole of the matter. All the gifts are needed, and without a team, there is no need for a leader nor will success be experienced. Let me always acknowledge people with words and actions. Help me to take time with people so that they always know I appreciate them. Thank You, Lord, for the people. Amen!

Notes/Reflections

R

Make God Your Priority

God must be your priority in everything. You are heirs to the throne of grace and joint heirs with Jesus Christ. You have the Word of God. *For the Word of God is living and powerful, and sharper than any two-edged sword, piercing even to the division of soul and spirit, and of the joints and marrow, and is a discerner of the thoughts and intents of the heart* (Hebrews 4:12). Jesus Christ is sitting on the right hand of the Father making intercession for you and making sure that everything you need is being dispatched to you. The Holy Spirit is residing within you, waiting to lead and guide you into all truth; grace and mercy are your companions, and the faithfulness and favor of God are upon you. Why go to other places and people? We are privy to all of this in God. He must be our priority. There is none greater than God.

The human side of us want to confer with flesh and blood, but nobody knows it all as God. We can discuss, but God must be our final stance. As a leader, there are some things that He is only going to tell you; then you can download it to others. He is Alpha and Omega. He is well qualified to run the affairs of your personal life and give perfect insight into the ministry that you have been called to lead with creativity and fresh insight. Everything!

<u>Prayer</u>

Father, I yield and surrender myself anew to You. I acknowledge today that it is You that I need in every aspect of my life. Anything in me that has a greater importance than You, please move it out of the way. I need You Father for my life and to be a leader to and with Your people. I need You Father above all things. I love You, Lord. Amen!

Notes/Reflections

S

Walk by Faith

We walk by faith and not sight. A lot of what you are called to do you will not see it or see you being the one to do it. But as God spoke to Moses and Joshua, so He will speak to you: *Have not I commanded you? Be strong and of a good courage; do not be afraid, nor be dismayed: for the Lord your God is with you wherever you go* (Joshua 1:9).

I am in awe knowing that God has called me and appointed me to the post of Pastor of Rehoboth Family Life Center. He always lets me know He has me and this is His doing, and He just needs me to listen and follow His lead explicitly. Do not try to figure it out and wonder why. Yes, it is you, so get before Him and continue to get all the things you need for your assignment.

Faith allows us to see us embracing all the wonderful things and moving in realms that our flesh cannot comprehend. This must be Spirit to spirit. Flesh cannot handle leadership roles in the Kingdom, and you will jump ship, always confused and just not want to do your assignment. You are it. Yes, you! Now say, "Yes me." Embrace your God given assignment of leading by faith and being blessed and being a blessing. See it all come alive by faith, creativity, wisdom, revelation, and boldness in the Holy Spirit.

Since I rededicated my life, it has not been ordinary; everything has been supernaturally driven. What about you? If you answer yes and even if you answered no, I believe from henceforth it shall be. This is a faith walk; exercise your faith walk and see all that is forthcoming as you move out of the box and let God be God in your life and the ministry that you have been called as a leader. Let faith paint the picture, then see it manifested upon the earth. Faith walk. Go beyond you, because it is beyond you. The best of you is still yet to come.

Prayers

Father God, I thank You for choosing me to be a part of Your plan of establishing Your Kingdom upon the earth. Help me to look beyond me and see You. Help me to not lean on my own understanding, doubts, fears, and insecurities and know that the greater one lives within me. Therefore, I can do all things that You are calling me to do. I am just so grateful to You, dear Lord. Amen!

Notes/Reflections

T

You Are Accountable to God

At the end of the day, you are accountable to God—not just to the Pastor, those you have been placed in leadership over, or better yet to lead, but God. The One who made the eyes can He see, and the One who made the ears can He hear? So at the end of the day have you done and said all that God has told you in the manner in which He told you? It can never be based on what someone else thought, wanted to do, or even disagreed because God gave the words and instructions to you, and He expects absolute obedient in what He has called. We as leaders must still stay open to suggestions, but they must be filtered through the Holy Spirit. Therefore, we should never be living or working independently of the Holy Spirit. Be sure to nurture that relationship so that you will know whether or not He is in agreement with you.

Not all good suggestions are for now, and some may never be used on what this church has been commissioned to do. Divine instructions must override suggestions if they do not fit in the framework of what God has called.

At the end of the day, is He pleased with you? Father God has the people and you, so He will give you the words to speak whether it is a yes or no. Listen for instructions.

What do you do when someone outright tells you that he or she disagrees with your directions? That has happened to me. Immediately I examined my reasoning behind the direction. Indeed if God has spoken this directive to me, I just say okay, but this is the way for it to be done. Now if I am making a suggestion that is not necessarily divinely given, I will say either let me mull it over and get back to you or okay if there is no push back in my spirit. As a leader, you must discern what place you need to be operating out of for a particular thing. Do not be afraid of hurting people because God loves them, but there are times you will have to say no because, at the end of the day, you are accountable to God.

Prayer

Father, help me to follow Your lead. Help me to clearly hear Your instructions and implement them as given. Help me not to be afraid of saying no and help me not to be a man pleaser when it does not agree with what You have spoken. Let me lead with love and say no with love when necessary and let it be received as such. At the end of each day, I want You to be pleased with me! Amen.

Notes/Reflections

_____

_____

_____

_____

_____

_____

_____

_____

_____

_____

_____

_____

_____

_____

_____

_____

_____

_____

_____

_____

U

Lead by Your Spirit and Not Your Emotions

Do not lead with your emotions, but your spirit. Emotions are funny and so unreliable when it comes to the truth of the matter. A lot of times emotions paint a picture that does not even exist. The Word tells us in 2 Corinthians 10:5, *"Casting down imaginations and every high thing that exalts itself against the knowledge of God, bringing every thought into captivity to the obedience of Christ."* Emotions are attached to feelings. Ministry or leading cannot be associated with how you feel. Emotions sometimes operate on our surroundings or environment. The sun is shining so brightly today, and I am happy. The day has been nothing but rain, which makes me sad so I am just going to stay in the house. Leading goes on regardless of our surroundings and anything else. Things have to get done regardless of how you feel. Therefore, I must operate out of my spiritual nature which is not moved by external conditions.

Some of my life changing events had real emotions attached to them. Therefore, I had to operate out of my spirit to know what to do. If I leaned my way to my emotions and those of others, I would have missed out on the most pivotal event of my life, my move from Philadelphia. My mother was crying, not understanding why and how I was moving; others had questions and doubts. I had no concrete things except I was being led by my spirit. I had no real emotions because I was not sure what this was, except it was God. Therefore, I had to remain focused on my spirit to know what to do. New life awaited me that could only be seen by my spirit. Thank you, Lord!

Stay in the reality of things and not what you would like it to be, or you will become frustrated, doubtful, and an emotional mess when reality shows itself. It was always there. Leadership calls for one to deal with the good, the bad, and the ugly of life with God. Acknowledge your emotions and when misplaced quickly get before God. You are not a robot with no emotions; just do not allow them to rule you because they will shade your judgment and decisions.

Prayers

Father, I thank You for life. Help me, dear Lord, not to be ruled by emotions, but by Your Spirit. Help me not to shut down my emotions where I feel nothing, but to acknowledge what I feel and give the situation over to You. I long to fully acquaint myself with the Holy Spirit that I may be led in all perfect truth. Thank You, Holy Spirit. Thou art welcome in my life to rule and abide. Amen.

Notes/Reflections

V

Leaders Serve

A leader should have excellent customer service skills and know who the customer is. The church is about God but for the people. The whole point of the plan of redemption and the crucifixion was for the people. If Jesus died for the people and thought them valuable enough to do so, then we must value the people as well.

As leaders, we should be instrumental in helping the people who come have a worship experience every time they grace the doors. How? By meeting their needs so that they can concentrate on the service without distractions.

Leaders should be well informed about the church in which they serve: location of rest rooms and children's church, logistics for Bible Study, vision and mission of the church, upcoming events, etc. Leaders should know who does what, so they will know who to go to for answers or where to direct people, instead of answering the people's questions quickly and impolitely.

Leaders go the extra mile to accommodate or answer questions and not just say, "No." Sometimes the bottom line answer is no, but a leader gives and is willing to give an explanation or a possible alternative.

Prayer

Father, You so loved the world that You gave Your only begotten Son so that we could be forgiven. Help me to care for what You deem precious and important—people. Help me to have balance when dealing with people and continue to be equipped with the necessary things to lead according to directives being given. In Jesus' name, Amen.

Notes/Reflections

W

Give Glory to God

To God be the glory! Where you lead is only by the awesomeness of God, so don't get geeked up on yourself and the possible accolades of others. Stay humble and give all glory to God at all times. *Pride goes before destruction and a haughty spirit before a fall* (Proverbs 16:18). Never think that you have arrived and have it all together. Be forever learning and receiving from God. Remember from where you came, who brought you, and who keeps you—God. To Him be glory, majesty, power, and dominion forever. Amen. By the grace of God go I.

Let God place and promote you. There is no need to blow your own horn. It is better to be called to the front from the back than to be sent to the back from the front. Let God choose your seat. Becoming content and satisfied with God causes us not to need the accolades of man and stops us from doing and saying things we shouldn't to get complimentary words.

Prayers

Lord God, help me to stay out of the way and forever put You first. I give You glory for everything I do and everything that I am. I realize that I am in Your plan and acknowledge now that it is indeed an honor and privilege. All honor and glory to You. Amen.

Notes/Reflections

X

Be Concise

Be concise in your instructions and comments. People will cut and paste your words, and some will be poor listeners. When they don't remember what you conveyed, they will fill in the blanks with their thoughts or assumptions. It is good to have procedures, instructions, or what is expected in written form as well as spoken to have everybody on the same page of what needs to be done.

Sometimes people will try to play one leader against another. Example: Someone calls one leader and ask if a certain thing can be done. The leader replies that it is probably not a problem and that he or she will run it pass another leader. The person mentions the situation to the second leader and states that the first leader already said it was okay. Later, when the two leaders talk about the situation, the second leader mentions that the person said that they had already given their approval. Not so. The Bible tells us to know those who labor among us. The person probably was not doing anything intentionally, but only gave part of the answer they received from the first leader to get what they wanted.

Let your "yes" be yes and your "no" be no. There are going to be times that a strong "No!" will be based on the instructions and procedures written for all. Discern, discern, and discern.

Prayers

Father, help me to be concise in my instructions and the words I speak so that it leaves no room for interpretation. Let me not be afraid to say "no" when it is against the way You said it should be done. Help me to know those who labor among us and those sent by the enemy to cause contention and strife. I pray a spirit of unity among us so that You command blessings forevermore. Amen.

Notes/Reflections

Y

Relationships

Watch how you handle and respond relationally to the opposite sex and nowadays even to the same sex. Never put yourself in compromising situations. Discern the intentions of people and even yourself. You and they are still in a body of flesh with no wings or halo. Someone should be present during meetings, know about your meeting, or be stationed outside of the door of your meeting. Everybody's intention is not pure. Watch your involvement with folks, especially going from one person to another in a relationship, because people will not take you seriously. And if you are married or in a relationship let in be known and be sure not to send mixed signals by what you say or do.

Dating: Are you ready for a relationship God's way and not the world's way, or the way you know? You truly need to learn a balance because relationships need time. Are you able to lead and have a relationship? Does the other person understand your role and responsibilities as a leader? Will they be supportive? Can you handle a relationship without being distracted?

Let not your good be spoken evil of. Flee even the appearance of sin. Watch, and watch you!

Prayer

Father, I pray that my heart is pure before You and everything I do and say is filtered through my spirit. Help me to discern where I should be. Help me to know and see the traps of the enemy, especially the people and places I think I know. Be pleased with my life, dear Father. Search me and find anything that is not of You that I may be all You have called me to be. In Jesus' name, Amen.

Notes/Reflections

Z

A Greater Work

Do not allow the words of others to penetrate and disturb your well-being and the flow of your spirit. People are going to say things that you do not like, to you and about you. Some statements or comments will be made one-on-one or in a group setting. Of course, check out you first to see if it was warranted; if not, keep it moving. If and when it penetrates, then go before God and get it up off of you. God will instruct you whether the issue needs to be discussed further with the person who put it out there. Know that the enemy will use anybody to disturb your well-being and your flow in the Spirit. Stay in tune with you and keep the flow open for a greater work. Offenses are going to come, of that, you can be sure, but it is how we respond that is most important.

I was at a gathering, and someone made a comment about me. When I think back, the person made several other negative comments and gestures toward me directly and indirectly. Therefore, I realized that some things besides me were going on with them. However, I did not like it and had to get before God, because I had to study and prepare for service the next morning. Part of all this was to get me out of the flow of the Holy Spirit. I acknowledged before God I did not like it but needed to move forward. And I did, even to be writing this entry the same day. To God be the glory!

Keep the channels of your life before the Holy Spirit open at all times. In the backdrop of all that God is calling you to do for the Kingdom, it is really not that important; so, keep it moving. There are things to be done for God, so stay open.

Prayer

Father, help me always to check me out first whenever anyone confronts me. If I am unclear on the matter, give me further wisdom on how to handle the situation. Help me not to take it on personally because then my spirit becomes clouded as with debris and I need to remain free to be about Your business. Help me to push through, forgive through, and love through the negative words of others for a greater work. Amen.

Notes/Reflections

_____
_____
_____
_____
_____
_____
_____
_____
_____
_____
_____
_____
_____
_____
_____
_____
_____
_____
_____
_____
_____
_____

AA

Wisdom to Lead

Do not feel like you always have to defend or further explain the position that God has told you to take. Everyone will not understand nor like it. When you bring clarity to a procedure or situation, do so, and back up off it. Do not feel the need to go around the mulberry bush with people about the same thing, especially when your stance has not changed. Of course, choose your words wisely and kindly because you do not want to offend anyone or injure them intentionally; although how they take what you say will determine whether they are offended or not. If they are offended or hurt, give the situation back to God and keep moving because there is Kingdom work that needs to be done.

As a leader, there are times you must confront situations. Remember when Jesus went into the temple and turned the table over and threw folks out. He told them, *"It is written, My house shall be called a house of prayer; but you have made it a den of thieves"* (Matthew 21:13). I do not like confrontations in the least, but I am not afraid to confront people and will do so when necessary for the benefit of all. *Do you not know that a little leaven leavens the whole lump?* (1 Corinthians 5:6b)

Ask God for wisdom as Solomon did that you may lead in the place God has called you to do. Do not allow people to pull you to their flow, but do as the Holy Spirit leads you! Remember, the enemy will use anything and anybody to get you off course. Declare not so! *For we do not wrestle against flesh and blood, but against principalities, against powers, against the rulers of the darkness of this age, against spiritual wickedness in high places* (Ephesians 6:12).

Prayer

Father, help me to be confident in what and how You have instructed me to do things. Give me the words to convey Your instructions to others. I understand that people are not always going to be receptive to all that You tell me to say. Help me to say and do what You instruct me to say and do anyway. Let me not argue with people or revile back at them, but have unconditional love and allow You to handle the situation. Let me never forget it is not the people, but the enemy is trying to get me distracted. I must do all to stay on Kingdom building. Amen.

Notes/Reflections

BB

Strengths and Weaknesses

As a leader, you must know your strengths and weaknesses. For the things that you are not familiar with or astute in, God will send you help to educate you or to take the particular task over. I have been blessed to experience both parts. We were blessed to have a well-established law firm do our 501(c)3 documents pro bono. That taught me a lot about the business and law side of ministry. Plus, I am so blessed to have Pastor Irma who is very technical and computer savvy and up on business/church laws.

Leaders need to be versed on not just ministry but business as well. Contracts will have to be negotiated for events, and budgets need to be approved to run the portion of the ministry for which you are responsible.

I am more of the people side and ask a lot of questions until I understand. I consider that a strength because there are times I see things that may affect the event or proper use of a building that the program lead person may not see. I am trying more not to shy away from technical stuff because these are the times in which we live. Do not ignore your weaknesses, but acknowledge them and move to do better because even if someone comes to take over that area, you need to know at least how it should work and what the results should be. For example, I know very little about the sound equipment, but I know when it is malfunctioning and when we can get a better sound out of it. Stay self-educated on various subjects.

Learn your style of leadership and get before God and let Him make it how He sees fit for the place in which you lead. I am a visionary and realize that fact so that I can do things from scratch; then someone else can run with it while He has me building the next thing. A good leader knows when and is not afraid to delegate. I am further learning this trait. I always feel that I would not ask anyone to do something I was not willing to do. A leader can do but needs to know when and to whom to delegate. Also, know the strengths and weaknesses of those in your group. *And we beseech you, brethren, to know them which labour among you* (1 Thessalonians 5:12a KJV). It is better to leave a position empty than to put someone there just for the sake of it because the job will not be done efficiently and it will become frustrating for you and them. The right person will come. Wait on them!

Prayer

Father, search me and help me to see me, my strengths, and my weaknesses. Help me to be the best me that You had in mind before the beginning of time. I pray that my gifts are stirred up today that I may be equipped to lead. Help me not to be afraid to ask questions. I pray for wisdom to do all that You have purposed me to do. I yield over to You, and my life is in Your hand. Help me not to become stagnated but to continue to grow in all things. In Jesus' name, Amen.

Notes/Reflections

CC

Character and Integrity

Character and integrity are paramount above gifting especially in you and those that you lead. Your job or responsibility is to help develop people with godly character who can be trusted. Know no man by what he talks about, but by his fruit, which is his actions. *You will know them by their fruits* (Matthew 7:16a).

Look for the undeveloped, raw gifting sitting among you waiting to be tapped. It is not always the obvious one who has always done a particular task, has a degree in it, and comes with a list of references. Let God show you who.

Prayer

Father, I ever stay before You that You may search me; if you find anything that is unpleasing rid me of it. My desire is to walk upright before You and Your people. Help me to know a person by their actions and not their words. I never want to be a hypocrite and become a castaway because I said one thing and did another. Let me stay ever before You Father that You may be pleased with me. Amen.

Notes/Reflections

DD

Don't Shrink Back

Do not shrink back, but embrace the leadership position you have been given and walk in the authority of it. There are certain things dispersed to leaders that God has called, to equip them to do what they have been called to do. I remember Apostle Saundra Hagans telling me now that I was walking in the role of a Pastor I would experience God in and on another level so I would be able to impart to the people. Indeed, I can say this has been my experience, and He continues to slowly open the curtain to reveal the mysteries of the gospel and divine revelation of the Kingdom. I am so grateful to God and realize without God opening things up to me the more; I would not be able to lead the people or speak life to them. I am totally dependent on Him.

Utilize all that divine authority gives you to lead and know you indeed have been given access to all you need.

Verily I say unto you, if ye have faith, and doubt not, ye shall not only do this which is done to the fig tree, but also if ye shall say unto this mountain, Be thou moved, and be thou cast into the sea; it shall be done. And all things, whatsoever ye shall ask in prayer believing, ye shall receive (Matthew 21:21-22 KJV).

Prayers

Father, help me not to shrink back but receive and walk in all that You have for my life. It is so not about me but all about You. You purposed to do Your will upon the earth and look for a submitted vessel to do so. If You go with me, I will go. If You say tell them, I will. All authority is in Your hands, and You give to us that we shall do greater exploits upon the earth that all may declare you are Lord.

Notes/Reflections

_____
_____
_____
_____
_____
_____
_____
_____
_____
_____
_____
_____
_____
_____
_____
_____
_____
_____
_____
_____
_____
_____
_____

EE

Looking for Easy

Leaders, true leaders, are not just willing to lead when the task is easy and does not require much to get the tasks completed. They are not faint at heart but are relentless even when, and especially when, the task calls for sacrifices of time, money, and energy. We want to be leaders because of what we think is glitz and glamor, but real leaders get in the trenches, sweat, and get dirty. Again, count the cost of being a leader.

I thank God for people that God has sent to help in the ministry, but before that, Pastor Irma and I knew what God told us had to be done and we did it. For our last retreat, six of us went up a day ahead to get things in order, but I remember for most of the previous retreats, she and I did the work ourselves because we were given the charge and it had to be done. Be willing to serve God and His people. Leading is not for the lazy and slothful. Ministry is work. Follow through to the end.

Do you not know that those who run in a race all run, but one receives the prize? Run in such a way that you may obtain it (1 Corinthians 9:24).

Prayer

Father, help me to be willing to do whatever it takes to do what You have assigned to my hand. Help me to hear Your instructions and move accordingly. Ministry is not easy; it is work. Help me not to be slothful or lazy, but be strengthened to do your bidding. Jesus went to the cross and bled willingly for me to be a part of Your plan of redemption. You have not required blood but commitment to see things to the end. Help me to be steadfast and not waiver to the end of the matter. Amen.

Notes/Reflections

FF

Be Ever Learning

Be ever learning. Never think you have arrived and have the know withal to do your assignment. *Study to show yourself approved to God, a workman that need not to be ashamed rightly dividing the word of truth* (2 Timothy 2:15 KJV). I read a lot, network, and visit places to stay abreast of what is going on in the world. You want to remain open to different ways of doing things, especially with God. You do not have the market on stuff no matter how good it is because it can always be and get better.

We serve such a creative God who has so many ways to get things done. Find out all that needs to be done in the place He has you. Do not be afraid to step into new territories. There is a whole world out there into which we have barely tapped. In college, I struggled writing essays until I wrote about something dear to my heart and I got my first B on a paper. Since then, I have written articles, books, words of encouragement, and now this leadership manual. Nobody but God is birthing out of me what He knows He has put in me. There is more. Do not put limits on your learning and becoming. Be ever learning about you.

<u>Prayer</u>

Father, You have given me gifts and talents. Help me to discover these things, become exercised in them, and then use them for the furthering of the Kingdom. Help me not be afraid to learn new things and do new things. I know that there is so much more to life and me. Let me become and stay open to new opportunities and unchartered areas even within me. I look forward to the newness in and outside of me. To God be the glory! Amen.

Notes/Reflections

GG

It Is God's Plan

As a leader, always be open and pliable in the hands of God, whenever there is a shift on the road, in ministry or in how things are done. Remember, you are in the plan of God who knows all things. This is not your plan nor are things done your way.

Several months after Rehoboth was started, there was a shift in the direction of our ministry. We were told by the Holy Spirit to focus on building the church. We had started out in 2005 as an outreach ministry, so the women's ministry, benefit concert, 5 a.m. prayer, and my prophetic writing of "Lifeline" ceased within a matter of days. Pastor Irma and I would be talking about something surrounding these areas, and before our conversation ended, we knew in our spirits that we needed to stop the activity. I had a special attachment to the women's ministry, "Arise," because that was the first portion of ministry that had been birthed. We thought about waiting until after our annual retreat to end the women's Bible Study since we were close to the time, but things kept evolving, and we knew the time was now. God did not allow any fanfare or parting events, but just an email to inform participants and supporters that we were obeying the voice of God and the outreach ministry and events were no longer going to be done, while we built Rehoboth Family Life Center. We had to make the sudden shift with He that was in control.

Keep your head and emotions out of the picture when there is a shift and just obey the divine instructions given to you. Stay open, stay open, stay open to God! There is always a bigger picture working—from glory to glory.

> *"For My thoughts are not your thoughts, nor are your ways My ways," says the Lord. "For as the heavens are higher than the earth, so are My ways higher than your ways, and My thoughts than your thoughts"* (Isaiah 55:8-9).

Prayer

God, I realize that I am a vessel in Your plan. I do not know how things are to play out. Therefore, I must listen for instructions and move accordingly. Help me to stay out of my head and allow my spirit to lead and guide me. I trust You on my journey whichever way it takes me as long as I know You are there with me. Your plan is what I so desire for my life. Amen!

Notes/Reflections

HH

Keep Moving Forward

A good leader is progressive, always moving forward and only reflecting in the past for principles learned from previous lessons. We do it this way because we have always done it that way. Or, this is the way we did it at my old church. No! Allow new things to be birthed in the place you lead and remain open to it.

The place where the church is currently located is owned by a fellowship community; whenever we ask for something their response has been from the very beginning, "We have never done that before, but who said we can't." Stay open to new ways of doing things. We serve a creative and progressive God, and we must always follow His lead. There is just so much more to do in the earth. Stay open and move forward. Press! *Old things have passed away; behold, all things have become new* (2 Corinthians 5:17b).

Prayer

Father, help me to move forward and progressively with You. Please do not allow me to become locked in the past or even in the present, but always looking ahead for the new things. Get the glory out of my life, in Jesus' name. Amen.

Notes/Reflections

II

Show Respect

Respect those that are in the group you are leading. Do not confuse the facts. You are the leader and not better than they are. Do not talk down to or be condescending to make you look better or more. Do everything and say everything unto the Lord. You respect them, and they will respect you. Respect is reciprocating. Isn't it all about God for the people? Then treat them as such. *And just as you want men to do to you, you also do to them likewise* (Luke 6:31).

Prayer

Help me to respect what is dear to You Father, your people. You gave the best for them. Now help me to give the best of me (which is You in me) to them. They are so important to You, and You have proven it to be so. Let it be with me as well. Amen.

Notes/Reflections

JJ

Do Not Compromise

Do not compromise your stance for the liking or acceptance of people. There is always going to be someone who will disagree or want it done their way for their individual benefit and not for the good of the whole. You must keep your focus clear on the what, when, and how that God has given you. Stand your ground, use tact, and treat people gingerly. You do not want to hurt or wound anyone, but you must do things the way you have been instructed to do. Know that people are at different faith walks and one of your tasks as a leader is to help them become mature and steadfast in their walk. When you do not move, know they have to deal with God, not you.

Jesus did nothing of Himself, but only what He heard from His Father:

Then said Jesus to them, "When you lift up the Son of Man, then you will know that I am He, and that I do nothing of Myself; but as My Father taught Me, I speak these things" (John 8:28).

Saul lost his kingship because of compromise and disobedience:

> *"But the people took of the plunder, sheep and oxen, the best of the things which should have been utterly destroyed, to sacrifice unto the Lord your God in Gilgal." So Samuel said: "Has the Lord as great delight in burnt offerings and sacrifices, as in obeying the voice of the Lord? Behold, to obey is better than sacrifice, and to heed than the fat of rams. For rebellion is as the sin of witchcraft, and stubbornness is as iniquity and idolatry. Because you have rejected the Word of the Lord, He also has rejected you from being king"* (1 Samuel 15:21-23).

Prayer

Father, help me to obey Your instructions. Help me always to have a teachable spirit and filter what is spoken through the Holy Spirit. I want You to be pleased with me, and Your people need to see me standing in what I say are Your instructions. Thank You, Father. Amen.

Notes/Reflections

KK

Do Not Lead in the Blind

Know what you have been called to do and who has called you. You cannot lead in the blind. Knowing that it was God causes you to stay on your face before Him to receive encouragement, direction, and wisdom. It is and must be about God and the people you lead. It is not about anything or anyone else except God being priority in everything that you do and say. Is He pleased with you?

And He spoke a parable unto them, can the blind lead the blind? Will they not both fall into the ditch? (Luke 6:39) Only God knows the paths you are to travel, so listen and then obey.

Prayer

Father, first I thank You for choosing me to lead Your people. Keep me from stumbling and falling. You know the way I take. Help me to put nothing before You, listen for Your voice, and follow explicitly. I am nothing without You and can do nothing without You. But with You all things are possible. I need You each and every day to be my priority. Thank You now. In Jesus' name, Amen.

Notes/Reflections

I Call Forth the Leader in You

I am just so in awe, and I have learned so much of the necessary principles of leadership given by God. For six weeks, every day but Sunday, He gave me the entries that you have just read. I pray that you are now even better equipped to walk in divine leadership in the place in which God has or is calling you.

I pray you go forth, using the God-given principles and God-breathed word on your gifts for the furthering of the Kingdom. The people are waiting. The word and promises have preceded you, and already some things are in place to be further implemented by you. You have been called to the plan of God. Remember to always consider and treat it as an honor. Now go forth and lead!

Apostle Shirley J. Jones

Apostle Shirley J. Jones is a Pastor, Preacher, Teacher, Author, and Visionary. She has a heart and love for God and His people. She serves as the Senior Pastor of Rehoboth Family Life Center (RFLC) in Upper Marlboro, Maryland. RFLC is a church dedicated to the healing of families to heal the nations. The Lord has given her the charge to make disciples; help them identify their spiritual gifts and set up platforms of opportunities for their gifts to be exercised, and then release them into their divine destiny.

As an Author, she has written *"Lifeline: When God Speaks" Volumes 1 and 2.* Both books were was birthed out of times of God speaking life to her so that she could speak to others. Accompanying the books is a four-song worship compact disc, *"Lifeline: Songs of Encouragement."* The songs on the CD were birthed out of times she spent in prayer and from her desire to express her gratitude to the Lord. (Rev. Leslie Randolph-Moss, a psalmist, added music to the lyrics and sang the songs for the CD). These are songs no one else had sung because they were unto the Lord! She is also a writer for *Hidden Strength Newsletter* where she submits articles quarterly to encourage and give hope to those who may have lost their way.

Apostle Jones hosts a broadcast, *"Lifeline,"* the first Monday of every month at 7:00 p.m. on *When Christian Speaks Blog Talk Radio.* The broadcast allows her to share the gospel and set up a platform for others to come and share words of life and encouragement. It airs throughout the world.

To inquire about book signings, book reviews, speaking or ministry engagements, please contact:

Shirley J. Jones
P.O. Box 3005
Crofton, MD 21114

sjj@shirleyjjones.com

(443) 306-1520

Or visit www.shirleyjjones.com

For more information about this book, please contact:

Kingdom Living Publishing
P.O. Box 660
Accokeek, MD 20607

publish@kingdomlivingbooks.com

(301) 292-9010

Or visit www.kingdomlivingbooks.com

www.ingramcontent.com/pod-product-compliance
Lightning Source LLC
Chambersburg PA
CBHW060909280326
41934CB00007B/1254